# Read, Search & Find®

**Kidsbooks®**

Illustrations Copyright © 2012, Orpheus Books Ltd
2 Church Green Witney, Oxon OX28 4AW

Illustrated by Peter Dennis (Linda Rogers Associates)
Written by Mandie DeGagne

Printed in China

011502026JS

**Visit us at www.kidsbooks.com**

# Contents

# Introduction

Ahoy, mate! Get ready to sail the high seas for a grand adventure in the Age of Sail.

**PIRATES** takes you on a journey to a time when bands of buccaneers swarmed the waterways on large wooden vessels. Colorful illustrations and Search & Find® activities bring their world to life. You'll peek belowdecks and into the lives of pirates—how they dressed, what they ate, and where they slept. Join the crew in battle, visit a pirate city, dive for treasures nearly lost in a shipwreck, and more!

In the back of this book, curious sailors will discover the **Find Out More** section, where you can learn more about life at sea and uncover even more pirate knowledge.

So pack your sea bag and prepare yourself to **Read, Search & Find®** all there is to know about pirates!

# Building a Ship

Pirates roamed the seas during a time called the Age of Sail, when merchants and navy sailors traveled on large wooden sailing ships. These vessels came in many shapes and sizes and were built in special places called shipyards. Materials for shipbuilding were brought to the yard and transformed into galleons, brigantines, frigates, or schooners by hundreds of expert tradesmen.

### Blueprints
These detailed drawings included specific instructions for building the ship.

## Search & Find®

- ☐ Barrels (2)
- ☐ Dogs (2)
- ☐ Falling men (2)
- ☐ Horse
- ☐ Ladders (8)
- ☐ Sculptor

**Find Out More**
on page 26

### Pitch
Carpenters called shipwrights mixed this dark, sticky substance with rope fibers to make oakum, which sealed the seams between planks on a ship to make it waterproof.

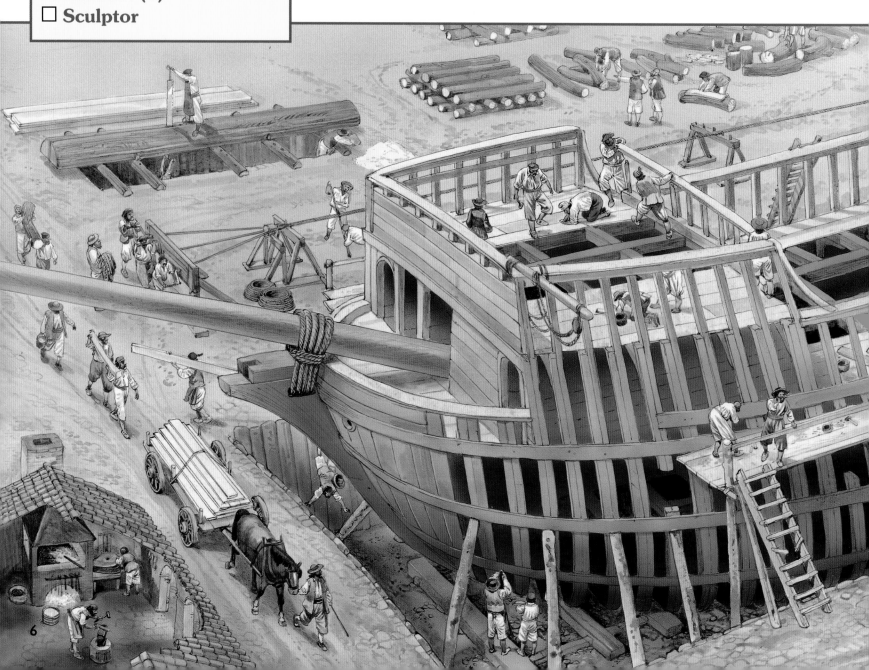

## Planks
Lumber was carefully shaped by carpenters into planks that formed the decks and hull of the ship.

## Blacksmith
Blacksmiths created metal ship fittings, like bolts and hinges, by heating iron and shaping it with special tools.

## Wooden Logs
Trees were chopped down in forests and delivered to the shipyard. The most popular wood for shipbuilding was oak, with pine for the masts.

## Rope-making
Natural fibers were twisted into long strands of rope. Sailors used rope on ships for rigging and controlling the sails.

7

# The Bow

Pirates were seagoing thieves. They captured merchant ships filled with treasures and valuable items like sails, ammunition, and spices. Before becoming pirates, most of these men worked as sailors who joined pirate crews when their own ships were overtaken. The bow, or forward portion of the ship, included areas needed for the crew's daily living, like places to cook, eat, and sleep.

## Figurehead
The figurehead was a decorative wood carving that was mounted to the prow, or forward-most portion of the bow.

## Parrot
Pirates who visited tropical islands brought back these colorful birds to keep as pets, give as gifts, or sell in the marketplace.

## Search & Find®

- [ ] Bananas
- [ ] Chicken
- [ ] Fiddle
- [ ] Heart
- [ ] Monkey
- [ ] Pigs (2)
- [ ] Prisoner

## Cannon

These large bronze weapons were fired from the gun deck through holes in the hull called gun ports.

## Hammock

Sleeping space was limited, so pirates slept in hammocks. These cloth beds were tied up with rope on the gun deck of the ship.

## Pistol

Pirates carried multiple pistols at all times. Moisture could prevent these guns from firing, so they always had spares.

## Cook

The important job of feeding the crew was often assigned to one of the disabled seamen. Long John Silver, from *Treasure Island*, was a sea cook.

## Small Arms Chest

*Arms* is a word used for weapons. Small arms, like pistols and muskets, were kept in wooden storage boxes on the gun deck.

**Find Out More** on page 27

# The Stern

Life at sea could be harsh, with extreme weather conditions leaving pirates wet and cold for days on end. Hard work on deck was often dangerous and required a great deal of strength and skill. The stern of the ship, or back portion, included storage spaces, officers' cabins, and parts used to steer the vessel.

### Rudder

This wooden flap was attached to the stern on hinges. It altered the ship's direction when moved left or right by the tiller, a long wooden pole connected to the whipstaff.

### Captain

A pirate captain was the leader of his crew. Most captains were experienced seamen with strong personalities.

### Whipstaff

When moved from side to side, this lever moved the rudder left or right. This caused the ship to change direction.

### Anchor

This heavy metal object was attached to a long cable and lowered to the sea bottom to hold a ship in place.

### Bilge Pump

Pirates used this pump to remove water that collected at the bottom of the ship. The water came in from rainstorms, large waves, and small leaks in the hull.

### Silk Sash

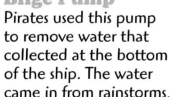

Worn around the waist or over the shoulder, these strips of cloth were convenient places to tuck or tie weapons.

Find Out More
on page 27

# Search & Find®

☐ **Barrels (15)**
☐ **Cat**
☐ **Duck**
☐ **Hourglass**
☐ **Lanterns (3)**
☐ **Mice (5)**

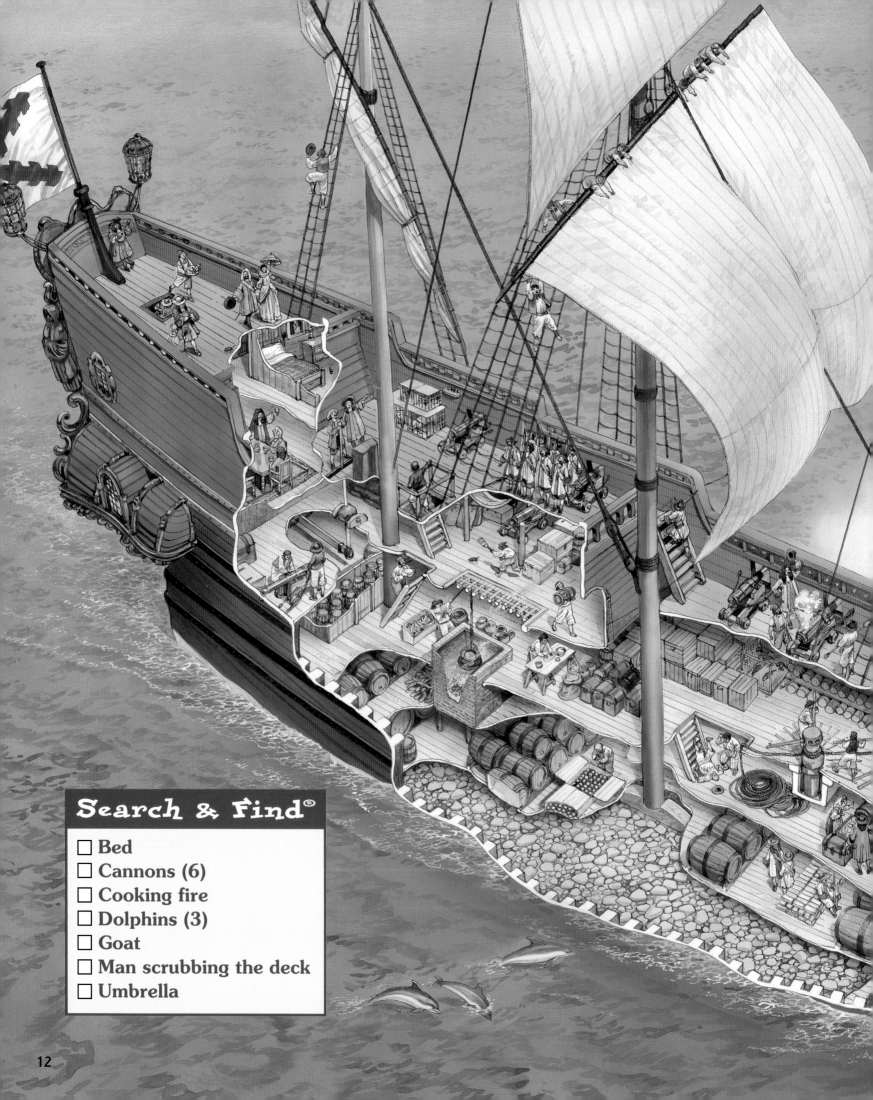

# Search & Find®

- ☐ Bed
- ☐ Cannons (6)
- ☐ Cooking fire
- ☐ Dolphins (3)
- ☐ Goat
- ☐ Man scrubbing the deck
- ☐ Umbrella

# Galleon

Galleons were bulky Spanish merchant ships that sailed to ports along the coastline around the Caribbean Sea, which was known as the Spanish Main. While anchored at these ports, galleons were filled with gold, silver, spices, gems, and other valuable materials to be brought back to Spain. These treasure ships were very appealing targets for bands of greedy buccaneers.

### Spare Sails

If a sail was torn in a storm or battle, the crew would replace it with one of the extras kept in storage.

### Gold

This precious metal was mined in South America and brought by pack animals and ships to the Spanish Main for trade.

### Capstan

This wooden cylinder was pushed with wooden levers to wind rope, raise the anchor, or lift heavy objects over the side of the ship.

### Shrouds

These long bands of netting provided support for the masts and allowed crewmembers to climb up to the sails.

### Rammer and Sponge

This tool had a wooden block on one end to push the gunpowder and ammunition into the barrel of a cannon. The other end was a soft piece of wet material used to clean the cannon after it was fired.

### Cooking Fire

The cooking fire was enclosed in brick and fed with dry wooden logs. It was extinguished in choppy seas and in battle to prevent the ship from catching fire.

### Crow's Nest

Sailors used this platform built high up on the mast to keep a lookout for land and enemy ships.

**Find Out More** on page 28

# A Battle!

With black flags hoisted and cannons blazing, pirates were fearsome enemies. Buccaneers were fully armed with pistols, swords, hand grenades, and muskets. Pirate crews preferred to come alongside their target and battle in close quarters. Groups of men, called boarding parties, were sent in small boats to climb aboard the target vessel. Pirates stole treasure and ship supplies, and forced men with special skills to join their crew.

## Musket
This type of gun was loaded with gunpowder and small lead balls through the end of the barrel, or muzzle.

## Pirate Surgeon
Sailors were vulnerable to serious injuries and would rely on the ship's surgeon to mend their wounds. If a surgeon was unavailable, the ship's carpenter might fill the role.

## Peg Leg
If a pirate's leg was lost in battle, surgeons would try to replace it with a wooden leg, or peg leg.

## Swivel Gun
This gun was a small cannon mounted on the ship's deck rails.

## Sword Fight
If pistols weren't firing or were out of ammunition, pirates could count on their cutlasses in close combat.

## Jolly Roger
The Jolly Roger is the black pirate flag, raised to intimidate enemies. The classic image is a black flag with a white skull and crossbones, but there were many variations.

**Find Out More** on page 28

14

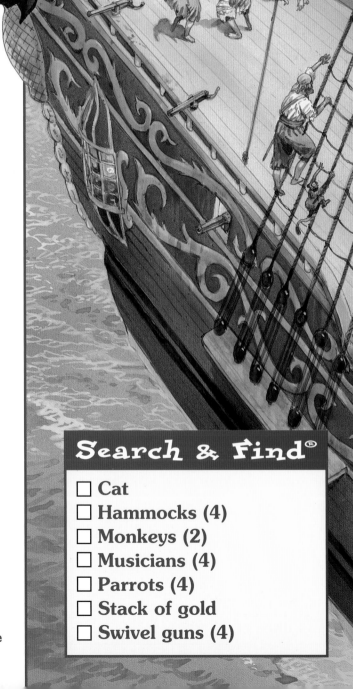

## Search & Find®

- ☐ Cat
- ☐ Hammocks (4)
- ☐ Monkeys (2)
- ☐ Musicians (4)
- ☐ Parrots (4)
- ☐ Stack of gold
- ☐ Swivel guns (4)

# Dividing the Spoils

When pirates joined a crew, they were required to sign the pirate articles of the ship. This written code gave instructions for living life at sea. According to the articles, pirate crews decided how to split up their loot before embarking on their voyage. Each pirate went into battle knowing he would receive a certain share of the riches they plundered.

**Oars**
Sailors used these wooden paddles to maneuver a boat by hand.

## Search & Find®

- ☐ Captain
- ☐ Coconuts (2)
- ☐ Chickens (6)
- ☐ Dogs (2)
- ☐ Flag
- ☐ Ladies (2)
- ☐ Mugs (2)

**Palm Tree**
Pirates would encounter these tall trees in tropical destinations. The coconuts that grow on palm trees contain nourishing white meat and fresh coconut water.

## Roasted Meats

The term *buccaneer* comes from a French word meaning *roasted meats*, because the original buccaneers were known for this type of cooking and eating.

## Ship's Boat

Large ships carried these small boats powered by oars or a sail that were used to board other ships or to go ashore.

## Powder Keg

A powder keg was a wooden barrel used to store gunpowder. It was kept in a cool, dry place to prevent it from exploding.

## Exotic Clothing

Pirates collected clothing from faraway lands on their journeys. They incorporated velvet pants, fancy jackets, and other accessories into their own wardrobes.

## Sea Chest

A sailor's sea chest was a wooden box that held all of his personal belongings.

**Find Out More**
on page 29

# Shipwreck

When we look at a shipwreck, we see the remains of a sunken vessel. The ship may have been struck down in battle, destroyed in a storm, or broken apart in a crash on a rocky shoreline. One of the most famous shipwrecks was the sinking of the pirate ship *Whydah* in 1717 off the coast of Cape Cod, Massachusetts. The *Whydah*'s treasures remained on the seafloor for more than 250 years before they were discovered.

## Search & Find®

- ☐ Crabs (6)
- ☐ Divers (7)
- ☐ Jellyfish (2)
- ☐ Ladder
- ☐ Sharks (3)
- ☐ Sea stars (8)

### Treasure

Treasure came in many forms, including expensive jewelry, helmets, masks, gems, pearls, gold dust, and coins. Pieces of eight and doubloons were silver and gold Spanish coins of high value.

### Spar

These long wooden poles functioned as the ship's masts and yards. The bowsprit is a spar that extends from the bow of the ship.

### Sea Turtle

Sea turtles are marine reptiles that were once caught for food, but are now protected because of their status as endangered species.

## Octopus

These eight-legged sea creatures have no skeleton, making it easy for them to squeeze into tight spaces.

## Treasure Chest

A treasure chest is a wooden box filled with jewels and precious metals.

## Coral

Sunken ships in shallow tropical locations could become the framework for a coral reef.

**Find Out More**
on page 29

# Pirate Harbor

After successful expeditions, pirates often returned to safe places along the coast where they could dock their ships and spend their booty. These port cities were busy and filled with people of great wealth. One of the best known pirate harbor cities was Port Royal, Jamaica. The famous pirate captain Henry Morgan ruled as second-in-command to the governor of Port Royal for more than ten years.

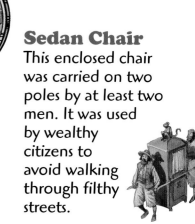

**Sedan Chair**
This enclosed chair was carried on two poles by at least two men. It was used by wealthy citizens to avoid walking through filthy streets.

## Search & Find®

- ☐ Bell
- ☐ Chandeliers (3)
- ☐ Drum
- ☐ Jolly Rogers (2)
- ☐ Men climbing a tree (2)

**Supply Shop**
Pirates could use their share of the spoils to purchase new clothing, weapons, or tools at the supply shops in town.

**Minuet**
A minuet was a popular ballroom dance that involved small steps and graceful movements between pairs of people.

**Street Vendor**
Street vendors made their livings by selling their products on the street to passersby.

**Town Watchman**
This guard had the important job of protecting the community by keeping a lookout for enemy ships and other suspicious activity.

## Tavern

Pirates returning from treasure raids would celebrate with their shipmates by drinking beer and eating food in the local tavern.

## Jail

Rowdy pirates who spent too much time in the taverns might have ended up in prison for their troublesome behavior.

**Find Out More**
on page 30

# Discovering a Shipwreck

Undersea archaeology is a form of science that allows experts to travel beneath the surface of the ocean and uncover pieces of history. Through careful observation of the location, position, and condition of a shipwreck on the seafloor, these men and women are able to put together a more detailed picture of the people who built and sailed the vessel.

## Stingray

This fish hides itself in the sand on the seafloor. A sharp stinger on the end of its tail is used in self-defense, so divers must be careful not to disturb these creatures.

## Diver

These people plunge themselves into a body of water to observe marine life and other objects found beneath the surface.

## Underwater Camera

Waterproof cameras are designed to withstand the moisture and pressure beneath the surface of the water.

## Search & Find®

☐ Barrel
☐ Baskets (3)
☐ Diver's scale drawing
☐ Dolphins (3)

## Lift Bags

Divers strap these undersea balloons to heavy artifacts. The bags are filled with air and float with the objects to the surface.

## Artifact

An artifact is a man-made object that reveals something significant about history or culture.

## Measuring Artifacts

Divers take very careful measurements of objects they find. Accurate calculations allow archaeologists to piece together the story behind the artifacts.

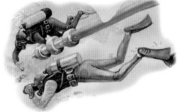

## Scuba Gear

This special equipment is designed to keep divers breathing while they explore the underwater environment.

## Grid

Archaeologists divide a site into small units by setting up a grid, or network of squares. They keep track of what they find in each section of the grid.

**Find Out More**
on page 30

# Pirate Ship Museum

A museum is a place where a special collection of objects is preserved and put on display to inspire and educate visitors. There are many types of museums, including art, history, and science. The pirate ship below proves that museums are not always located in a building! Artifacts are often protected behind glass cases, but when a ship becomes a museum, people are invited to climb aboard for a hands-on experience.

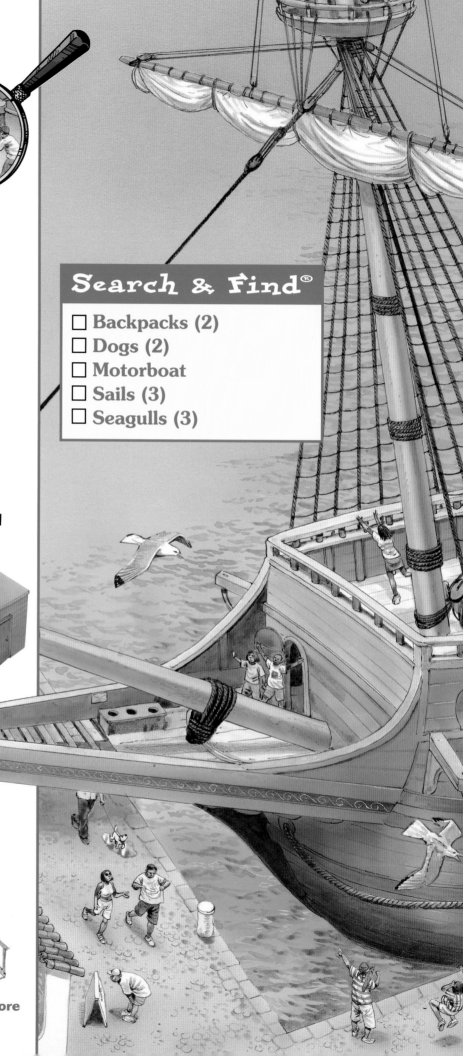

## Search & Find®

- ☐ Backpacks (2)
- ☐ Dogs (2)
- ☐ Motorboat
- ☐ Sails (3)
- ☐ Seagulls (3)

### Visitor's Guide
Museums often provide visitors with these pamphlets, which include information like safety rules and maps of the exhibits.

### Ticket Booth
This is where visitors pay a fee for admission. It is usually located at the museum entrance.

### Tourist
Tourists are people who have made a special trip to experience a new and different location.

### Docent
These people are knowledgeable about the museum and take groups on tours, explaining the exhibits.

### Gangplank
This ramp allows visitors to go aboard the ship.

### Sign
Signs are explanations of exhibits and can also be used to give directions to visitors.

**Find Out More**
on page 31

24

# Find Out More

## Building a Ship

The body of a ship is called the hull.

The right side of a ship (as you face the front) is called the starboard side. The left side is called the port side.

**Pitch, used to seal the seams in the hull, was made by mixing powdered charcoal with boiling pine sap.**

**The hammer and anvil were the blacksmith's main tools for shaping hot iron into metal parts.**

Cotton, hemp, and jute were the most common natural fibers used to make rope.

The Age of Sail (the 1500s to the mid-1800s) ended with the arrival of steam-powered ships.

# The Bow

Most pirates were young men in their twenties who did not have wives or children.

Women weren't sailors on wooden ships because of the hard labor and dangers involved.

Women were typically not welcome on ships at all, because they were considered a distraction.

Anne Bonny and Mary Read were two of the only known female pirates. They disguised themselves as men.

Pirates often had tan or sunburned skin from working out on deck, and many had scars or injuries from battle or accidents.

# The Stern

Pirates used many unique terms and phrases. The word *ahoy* was a way of saying hello. *Avast* meant to stop and observe.

Large wooden ships typically carried four to six anchors. They were lashed on the outer hull along the bow.

Sea chanteys were work songs that helped sailors perform repetitive tasks by keeping a steady rhythm.

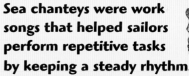

If a pirate told you to *strike your colors*, he was telling you to surrender by lowering your flag.

A corsair was a pirate from the Mediterranean Sea.

Buccaneers were pirates from the Caribbean Sea.

# Galleon

The Spanish conquered lands in Mexico and Peru, which contained some of the richest supplies of gold and silver in the world.

**Gold was sent back to Spain in the form of bars. Later it was converted to coins.**

Most pirates could be found along trade routes and where the weather was most favorable.

*Rigging* refers to all the ropes and pulleys used to hoist and lower a sail.

**Galleons were square-rigged ships, meaning that they hoisted large square sails.**

# A Battle!

Pirate flags could be black or red.

**Symbols on pirate flags included skulls and crossbones, skeletons, cutlasses, spears, daggers, cannonballs, bleeding hearts, and hourglasses.**

Sometimes pirates would hoist a false flag to trick an enemy into thinking they were a friendly ship.

**Pirate crews would sometimes fire a broadside to scare their enemies. This meant that they fired all of their cannons at once.**

In some battles, buccaneers tossed stink pots (filled with materials like dead fish and burning sulfur) onto their enemies' ships.

**Carpenters and barrel-makers from a captured ship were among the first sailors forced to join pirate crews.**

# Dividing the Spoils

Pirates usually dressed much like regular sailors, with loose-fitting shirts, canvas trousers, and handkerchiefs tied around their necks.

Pirate crews needed to careen their ships, which involved sailing their vessels onto a beach in order to clean and repair the hull.

Shipmates who broke the pirate code may have been marooned, or left alone, on a deserted island as punishment.

If they ran out of supplies, buccaneers went ashore to find food, water, and firewood.

# Shipwreck

Shipwrecks that occurred in fairly shallow waters may have been looted by people onshore.

The *Whydah* was a slave ship captured by the pirate captain Sam Bellamy.

More than 140 men perished in the *Whydah* shipwreck, including Captain Bellamy.

Shipwrecks like the *Whydah* are not easy to find. The ship was broken into small pieces and covered by sand over time.

The *Whydah* shipwreck was discovered by the undersea explorer Barry Clifford.

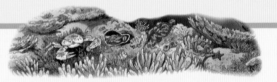

Coral reefs are built from the hard external surfaces of tiny marine animals called corals.

# Pirate Harbor

An earthquake destroyed Port Royal in 1692. Most of the city ended up underwater.

Edward Teach, known as Blackbeard, was captain of the ship *Queen Anne's Revenge*.

Jack Rackham, or Calico Jack, was a pirate captain who flew one of the best known Jolly Roger flags: a skull with two crossed swords beneath it.

**Two famous fictional pirates are Captain Hook from *Peter Pan* and Long John Silver from *Treasure Island*.**

# Discovering a Shipwreck

Marine archaeologists use sonar to determine the shape of the underwater landscape. Sound waves are sent to the bottom and bounce back at different speeds.

**Scale drawings can be done underwater with pencils on waterproof paper.**

Divers can communicate with one another by writing on plastic tablets called dive slates.

It can be too dark underwater to see or take clear pictures. Lamps that operate under the water are used to improve visibility and photo quality.

# Pirate Ship Museum

The curator of a museum is in charge of receiving, organizing, and protecting all of the museum's artifacts.

Restoration is the process of returning an artifact as close to its original form as possible—repairing or replacing faded or chipped paint, corroded metal, lost parts, and more.

**Museum educators create displays and signs that teach visitors about the objects in each exhibit.**

Museums use many techniques to preserve their collections. They may control the temperature and lighting in an exhibit where heat or bright light may damage the artifacts.

Most museums use a cataloging system, assigning numbers to each artifact in order to organize and keep track of the collection.